Deep in a Rainforest

Written by Gwen Pascoe
Illustrated by Veronica Jefferis

For a free color catalog describing Gareth Stevens' list of high-quality books and multimedia programs, call 1-800-542-2595 (USA) or 1-800-461-9120 (Canada). Gareth Stevens Publishing's Fax: (414) 225-0377. See our catalog, too, on the World Wide Web: http://gsinc.com

Library of Congress Cataloging-in-Publication Data

Pascoe, Gwen, 1942-
  Deep in a rainforest / by Gwen Pascoe; illustrated by Veronica Jefferis.
      p. cm.
    "First published in 1995 by ERA Publications, Australia"—T.p. verso.
    Summary: Illustrations and simple text highlight the colorful plants and animals of the rainforest.
    ISBN 0-8368-2149-1 (lib. bdg.)
    1. Rain forests—Juvenile literature. 2. Rain forest animals—Juvenile literature. 3. Rain forest plants—Juvenile literature. [1. Rain forests. 2. Rain forest animals. 3. Rain forest plants. 4. Color.] I. Jefferis, Veronica, ill. II. Title.
QH86.P37   1998
578.734—dc21   98-23889

North American edition first published in 1998 by
Gareth Stevens Publishing
1555 North RiverCenter Drive, Suite 201
Milwaukee, WI 53212 USA

Text © 1995 by Gwen Pascoe. Illustrations © 1995 by ERA Publications. First published in 1995 by ERA Publications, Australia.

Printed in the United States of America

1 2 3 4 5 6 7 8 9 02 01 00 99 98

Gareth Stevens Publishing
MILWAUKEE

2

Deep in a

rainforest,

the world

can be . . .

as

red

as . . .

7

as
orange
as . . .

as
yellow
as . . .

13

as

green

as . . .

as

blue

as . . .

as

purple

as . . .

27

as
bright
as . . .

. . . a
rainbow.